BRITAIN'S HERITAGE

Railway Stations

Tim Bryan

AMBERLEY

Acknowledgments

The author and publisher would like to thank the following people/organisations for permission to use copyright material in this book: The Railway Heritage Trust, Paul Childs, Hugh Llewellyn, STEAM: Museum of the GWR, Network Rail, Ben Brooksbank and the Sid Richards Collection. The cover image is courtesy of Paul Childs and the Railway Heritage Trust.

Every attempt has been made to seek permission for copyright material used in this book. However, if we have inadvertently used copyright material without permission/ acknowledgement we apologise and we will make the necessary correction at the first opportunity.

The author would particularly like to thank Andy Savage, Malcolm Wood and Claire Pickton at the Railway Heritage Trust for their assistance and guidance and allowing me access to their image collection, and to Paul Childs for his help in providing images from both his and the RHT archive. I am also very grateful to Hugh Llewellyn for providing me with photographs from his collection. Thanks are also due to Elaine Arthurs at the STEAM Museum for her assistance in sourcing pictures.

First published 2017

Amberley Publishing
The Hill, Stroud
Gloucestershire, GL5 4EP

www.amberley-books.com

Copyright © Tim Bryan, 2017

The right of Tim Bryan to be identified as the Author of this work has been asserted in accordance with the Copyrights, Designs and Patents Act 1988.

ISBN 978 1 4456 6900 7 (paperback)
ISBN 978 1 4456 6901 4 (ebook)

British Library Cataloguing in Publication Data. A catalogue record for this book is available from the British Library.

Printed in the UK.

Contents

1

Introduction

From the architecturally significant to the most austere and humble, railway stations of all shapes and sizes were one of the most prominent features of public life in cities, towns and villages all over Britain, until modernisation and closures swept many away.

Initially railway companies were primarily interested in generating income by carrying goods, not passengers, and the provision of facilities for travellers was rudimentary, using local inns or hotels to sell tickets at what were originally called 'stopping places'. With the opening of the Liverpool & Manchester and London & Birmingham railways in the 1830s the development of the station began in earnest, but it took some years for railways and their engineers to evolve a distinct style of building and layout.

As the number of railways and passengers grew, the design of stations began to take on a pattern that would be recognisable to us today. Buildings of all shapes and sizes were provided to accommodate ticket offices, refreshment rooms, lavatories and waiting rooms for first, second and third class passengers, left luggage, parcels and station offices.

Railway companies were able to employ some of the best architects of the age to build their new stations. The list of those who provided designs included some of the most famous, such as Isambard Kingdom Brunel, Sir John Fowler, David Mocatta, Sir George Gilbert Scott, George and Robert Stephenson, Francis Thompson and Sir William Tite. In addition, a

The northern terminus of the London & Birmingham Railway at Curzon Street, Birmingham. The main station building still survives and is to be part of a new terminal planned for the HS2 project. (Author's Collection)

KING'S CROSS STATION. G.N.R.

An Edwardian postcard view of the Great Northern Railway terminus at Kings Cross. (Author's Collection)

whole group of local architects not widely known in the railway world did valuable work for regional railway companies. In later years design work was undertaken by civil engineers whose names were not always recorded.

The most imposing stations were situated in large towns and cities, and most impressive of all were the London termini; terminals like Kings Cross, Liverpool Street, Paddington and Waterloo handled (and still handle) millions of long distance and commuter travellers every year. Their architecture and design remain a testament to the skill and daring of Victorian railway engineers and management. Elsewhere, cities like Birmingham, Manchester and Glasgow often had more than one important station handling express, cross-country and suburban traffic. These were often built on the same scale as the London termini, but many have not survived the dark years of railway modernisation and urban blight that followed.

Away from cities, the country station was an important part of rural life, providing a vital link for the movement of goods and passengers to and from the country. While the arrival of railways had transformed the lives of people living in urban areas, they also had a dramatic effect on the rural population. By the end of the nineteenth century there were few places not served by train and the opening up of previously remote places provided new markets for agricultural produce and ended the isolation of rural communities. The country station was at the centre of this change, whether it was a branch line terminus or a small wayside station on a main trunk line. Although lacking the grand architecture of the larger city terminal, the huge variety of styles and building materials used to build country stations make them just as interesting. Regrettably, many fine buildings were lost when closures prompted by the BR Modernisation Plan and the Beeching Report took place.

The railway station was also more than just a pure passenger facility; as it developed, the range of activities taking place within its precincts grew and, as well as the function of

Above: Glenfinnan Station on the West Highland line, pictured on 24 May 2012. The station now houses a railway museum, opened in 1991. (Railway Heritage Trust/Paul Childs)

Left: The Art Deco style tower of Surbiton Station, rebuilt by the Southern Railway in 1937. (Railway Heritage Trust)

The futuristic frontage of Birmingham New Street Station photographed while still under construction. The project to reconstruct the station was completed in September 2015. (Hugh Llewellyn)

serving travellers, many also included freight facilities, whether simply the handling of milk and parcels, or in the provision of more extensive goods yards and depots in smaller town or village stations. At larger city stations, in addition to the range of refreshment and dining rooms provided for passengers, many railway companies built large and lavish hotels for travellers wishing to break their journey.

Nineteenth and early twentieth-century railway architects built stations in a dazzling variety of styles, including Arts & Crafts, Gothic, Neo-Classical, Tudor and more besides; their twentieth-century successors had less opportunity or budget to continue at the same pace. The longevity of their creations is a tribute not only to their skill and flair, but also the quality of materials and workmanship employed. There is little doubt that railways 'built to last', and despite the best efforts of later railway management and planners, many historic stations survive. There has also in recent years been something of a renaissance in station development with major new stations being built or rebuilt. This work has been supported by the work of the Railway Heritage Trust and with careful conservation and sympathetic redevelopment many heritage stations can and will serve the modern railways' needs for many years to come.

2
Station Development

To begin with, little thought was given to station design. Perhaps unsurprisingly, passenger facilities were based on the transport they were shortly to usurp – the horse-drawn coach. Away from bigger towns and cities at wayside stations, passengers bought their tickets from a nearby coaching inn and later, as services developed, from a simple small building housing a booking hall and waiting room. There were no platforms, a simple levelled area next to the track instead serving as the place where passengers could step up into the waiting railway carriage.

The opening of the Liverpool & Manchester Railway in 1830 marked not only the completion of the world's first intercity railway, but also the introduction of what might properly be called the first railway station. The short-lived terminus at Liverpool Crown Street contained most of the basic features that survive in stations today; passengers arriving by carriage or omnibus bought tickets in a large space also used as a waiting room and joined their train from a platform protected from the elements by a train shed. Both Crown Street and the Liverpool Road terminus in Manchester were quickly replaced by larger, more central stations by the mid-1840s, and while Crown Street was rebuilt, Liverpool Road station survives today as part of the Manchester Museum of Science & Industry.

Impressive though these facilities may have seemed, the new stations were largely wooden in construction and many were 'an assortment of scruffy, draughty and uncomfortable' sheds or huts, as historians Richards and McKenzie wrote in 1986. As yet there was no defined style, but the opening of the London & Birmingham Railway in 1838 saw the construction of two impressive neoclassical station buildings at either end of the new line.

This 2006 view of Darlington clearly shows one of the three spans of the overall roof provided by the North Eastern Railway when the station was built in 1880 as well as some impressive cast-iron fencing around the subway and stairs. (Railway Heritage Trust)

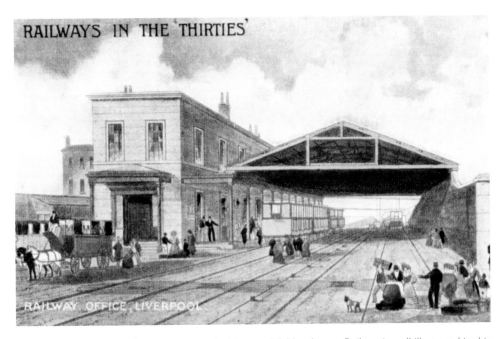

The simple design of the first stations on the Liverpool & Manchester Railway is well illustrated in this postcard view of Liverpool Crown Street in the 1830s. (Author's Collection)

Although the London & Birmingham had Robert Stephenson as its engineer, the design of both its London terminus at Euston and its Birmingham station at Curzon Street was the work of architect Philip Hardwick. The great 'arch' (technically a propylaeum) at Euston, completed in 1837, formed a 'grand entrance' to the station along with six smaller pavilions used as offices screening off a double-span steel train shed. Costing £35,000, the Euston Arch was controversial from the start, the architect Pugin describing it as 'a piece of Brobdignaggian absurdity'. At Birmingham, rather than repeat the Doric arch design, Hardwick created a grand neoclassical frontage complete with Ionic columns, incorporating a booking hall, refreshment rooms and offices.

Did you know?

Although railway stations are seen as a potent symbol of the Victorian age, their origins can be traced to the reign of King George III. There is still debate about what might be the earliest station. Little is known about the facilities built for the Surrey Iron Railway at Mitcham in 1803 and at Swansea for the Swansea & Mumbles Railway four years later, but they were probably used predominantly for goods traffic. The first public railway, the Stockton & Darlington, opened in 1825 and when it began carrying passengers in September that year there were no proper stations, as initially the railway focussed its efforts on coal traffic. The first purpose-built station at Darlington was not built until 1842.

Hardwick's iconic arch at Euston as recorded by the artist and engraver J. C. Bourne. The train shed can be seen in the distance behind the arch. (SSPL)

The adoption of styles other than the neoclassical stations favoured in larger cities was a reflection of the massive expansion of railways during the 'Railway Mania' period of the 1840s when more than 6,000 miles of new railway were authorised by Parliament. Isambard Kingdom Brunel, appointed as engineer to the Great Western Railway in 1833, utilised Tudor and Jacobean styling in both smaller wayside stations and larger city locations. The western terminus of the Great Western at Temple Meads in Bristol was built in grand Tudor fashion with a three-storey façade housing passenger facilities and a boardroom. Behind this was an impressive wooden train shed with a mock hammerbeam roof built in the medieval manner.

The Tudor style was used elsewhere to great effect; in 1848, T. K. Penson produced a two-storey station at Shrewsbury that was made even more impressive in 1903–4 when it was underpinned and another storey added. Shrewsbury was a joint station, sharing traffic from Great Western and the London & North Western railways. Another joint station at Carlisle Citadel – one of the most important junctions on the British network – had seven different railways using its lines by 1880. Sir William Tite's Tudor design featured a buttressed entrance arcade and clock tower when built in 1847.

Many rural stations were subsequently built in the Jacobean style, some differing from Tudor designs by featuring characteristic Dutch gables and rounded windows. In East Anglia, some of the best examples of this style by architect Frederick Barnes for the Ipswich & Bury Railway in the mid-1840s survive in locations like Bury St Edmunds, Needham Market and Stowmarket.

A further building style characterised the Railway Mania era and after; Italianate was heavily influenced by sixteenth-century Italian architecture. Larger stations tended to be built in what was described as the 'Palazzo' style, with large symmetrical facades often featuring arcades of arches and impressive *porte-cochères*. Examples of these fronted large train sheds include Thompson's North Midland Railway station at Derby, completed in 1841, and his design for Chester, completed in 1848. The latter also featured campanile-like turrets or clock towers that were often a feature of Italianate style stations.

Above: Behind the Tudor-style station building, Brunel's station at Temple Meads in Bristol also featured a 220-foot-long impressive train shed with a roof span of 74 feet. The station is now a conference centre and events venue. (STEAM: Museum of the GWR)

Below: Bury St Edmunds, built for the Ipswich & Bury Railway in 1846, originally had an overall roof but this was replaced by the Great Eastern Railway with the more modest platform awning seen in this photograph. (Railway Heritage Trust/Paul Childs)

Cupar, opened in September 1847 by the Edinburgh & Northern Railway, provides a good example of the Italianate style used on railways all over Britain in the nineteenth century. (Railway Heritage Trust/Paul Childs)

A variation was the 'Italian Villa' – a more modest design reflecting smaller rural homes built during the Renaissance. Featuring low-pitched roofs, exposed brick or stonework rather than stucco, round-topped windows and towers, so many country stations were built to this pattern that it was called the 'English Railroad Style' and examples appeared all over the network.

By the 1860s, the 'Railway Mania' era was well and truly over and most main lines had been completed, although branch lines continued to be built, serving areas previously ignored by railways in the early years. Traffic continued to grow and railways found themselves having to extend or rebuild stations to cope with increased business. Forty years after the opening of the Stockton & Darlington, the design of a railway station had finally become more standardised; a basic station might include two platforms usually linked by a footbridge, booking office and waiting rooms, lavatories and offices.

Did you know?

As the nineteenth century progressed, the number of architectural styles employed by railway engineers grew further, and the increasing use of Gothic Revival architecture promoted by John Ruskin and Augustus Pugin in churches and public buildings inevitably led to more stations of this design appearing. Gothic was characterised by pointed arches in windows and doors, steeply pitched roofs with decorated bargeboards and church-like towers. While earlier stations were built from local stone, by the late 1860s decorative polychromatic brick was the vogue, complemented by bands of different coloured tiles on roofs.

Above: Newark Castle Station, pictured in 2016. The classically styled station was built in 1846 for the Midland Railway. (Railway Heritage Trust/Paul Childs)

Below: A 1970s view of Shrewsbury Station. The Tudor design by T. K. Penson also features 'pepper-pot' chimneys and decoration. The area in front of the main building was lowered when an additional storey was added early in the twentieth century. (Hugh Llewellyn)

One of the decorative lamps situated around Great Malvern Station, photographed in 2011. (Railway Heritage Trust/Paul Childs)

Passengers waiting for trains in the early days of railways had to shelter from the elements in waiting rooms or under large train sheds. The development of glazing systems, most notably the one invented by Joseph Paxton and used in the 1851 Crystal Palace, enabled architects to build not only large overall roofs for major terminals, but also smaller platform awnings for wayside stations. The ridge and furrow system of roofing became extremely popular across the network, most notably on the Midland Railway. Cast-iron columns featuring decorative brackets or capitals, such as those at Great Malvern on the GWR, supported roof canopies.

By 1880, the network was largely complete with the exception of main lines like the Great Central and Settle & Carlisle, built just before the start of the twentieth century. Rather than building more new lines, railways instead concentrated on upgrading existing stations that had become outdated and cramped. Many were rebuilt in a grander manner; stations at Norwich, Reading and Slough were extensively rebuilt in a style inspired by French Renaissance architecture. By the 1890s, however, many railways like the GWR had evolved 'standard' building styles for their stations that used mass-produced building materials like brick, steel and timber that, while lacking the flair of earlier years, were distinctive and cost effective.

Before the Great War there were a number of additional major station rebuilding projects, such as those at Aberdeen, Birmingham Snow Hill and Glasgow Central, but the outbreak of war in 1914 ended further development. Between the wars the decline of the coal trade, industrial unrest, road competition and the Wall Street Crash hit the 'Big Four Railways' hard. Investment was limited and largely confined to new stations built for the Southern's

Above: The impressive façade of Norwich station is somewhat spoiled by the large numbers of cars parked in front of it. The rebuild of the station in 1886 cost £60,000. The clock in the central tower was supplied by Dixons, a Norwich company. (Author's Collection)

electrification project, the London Transport network and the rebuilding of GWR stations like Paddington, Bristol and Cardiff, funded by government loans. By 1935 Art Deco styling was widely used, with a cleaner, modern approach taken, with much use of new materials such as reinforced concrete, tiles and glass.

War and then nationalisation disrupted further development of stations and passenger facilities. Five long years of war, with its attendant bomb damage and lack of maintenance, made many stations look even more shabby and old-fashioned. Immediately after the Second World War, funds were required to repair and renew locomotives, rolling stock and freight facilities, and little was spent on new stations until 1955 when British Railways' Modernisation plan was published. The station at Potters Bar completed that year was followed by further new designs at Banbury in 1959, Manchester Oxford Road in 1960, and Coventry in 1962.

The new designs provided light and airy spaces for passengers and used reinforced concrete and glass, as well as more traditional building materials. Despite the bright future promised by the Modernisation Plan, the Beeching Report of 1963 signalled the dramatic reduction of the network and closure of many lines and stations, curtailing any large-scale redevelopment plans.

As well as the disappearance of many striking Victorian stations in the Beeching era, on the network that remained, changing operational and passenger needs meant that many older stations were not fit for purpose. There was little need for the large facilities provided in earlier times, and with many stations becoming unstaffed, buildings were swept away.

Above: An atmospheric evening scene at Leamington Spa Station pictured on 7 April 2014. (Railway Heritage Trust/Paul Childs)

Below: The original station serving Harlow was completed in 1842 to serve the village of Burnt Mill. When the new town of Harlow was built after the Second World War, the station was rebuilt by British Railways. (Railway Heritage Trust)

The futuristic scene at Reading Station, pictured while the station was still being redeveloped in 2013. The redevelopment, completed in 2014, cost £897 million and also included the construction of a flyover for trains west of the station. (Network Rail)

The BR era was also notable for some schemes that have subsequently been replaced; the rebuilding of Birmingham New Street in the 1960s was controversial at the time and the end result proved unsatisfactory for both passengers and staff. Less than forty years later the station was redeveloped once again.

It is an understatement to say that Britain's railway industry has undergone a huge change since the BR network was privatised in the 1990s. The debate about how railways are run and funded will continue, but there is no doubt that in recent years investment in both new and old stations, prompted by rapidly increasing passenger numbers, has led to some imaginative and stunning new designs.

3
London Termini

John Betjeman described London's railway termini as 'cathedrals of industrial architecture', writing about them in 1972 with affection and not a little sadness when many had been neglected and were in decline. Fortunately matters have improved and while there have been some casualties, millions of pounds of investment has transformed many into modern facilities that retain much of their architectural heritage.

The earliest London terminus was built south of the Thames; London Bridge served the capital's first railway, the London & Greenwich, and opened in 1836. Its subsequent history was complex as it grew to accommodate trains from the South Eastern and the London, Brighton & South Coast railways. Their stations sat next to each other with the picture further complicated by the addition of a new high level station in 1864 that enabled SER trains to run through to Charing Cross and Waterloo. Described as 'muddled and architecturally undistinguished' the elements were united in 1923 when they became part of the Southern Railway. Matters were not improved by wartime bomb damage and it was not until the 1970s that major investment took place at the station. A more radical redevelopment of London Bridge has taken place since 2009 with the removal of the listed train shed and retaining wall, the construction of a new concourse and additional platforms.

London's first intercity station was Euston. Behind Hardwick's grand arch Stephenson created two simple train sheds supported by cast-iron columns to handle traffic from the new London & Birmingham Railway. In 1846 Philip Hardwick and his son (also named Philip) designed the stunning Great Hall, a public space built in the Roman style. Josiah Stamp, General Manager

The incomplete skeleton of the Shard towers over the nineteenth-century train shed of London Bridge Station in October 2010. (Hugh Llewellyn)

The very undistinguished northern end of Euston station pictured in September 2009. (Hugh Llewellyn)

of the LMS until 1942, made no secret of his dislike of Euston and nearby St Pancras and made plans to sweep away both, but the Second World War saw this scheme shelved.

No further development took place until the 1960s when British Railways plans to build an entirely new terminal were revealed. Enlarging Euston would involve the demolition of the old station, including the Arch and Great Hall. Despite national protests, the controversial scheme went ahead and a new complex designed by R. L. Moorcroft – the architect for BR London Midland – replaced Hardwick and Stephenson's station. The modern frontage houses the concourse and public facilities, behind which eighteen platforms now sit underground, accessed by ramps.

From the beginning, the new Euston attracted criticism – its modernist design described as a 'hideous concrete box'. In 2007 plans were announced to redevelop the station again but were abandoned four years later. Current proposals for the new High Speed 2 (HS2) scheme to Birmingham and beyond will see a far more dramatic redevelopment with a twenty-four-platform terminal being proposed.

Euston was also originally intended to be the London terminus of the Great Western Railway. It had been planned that the GWR and London & Birmingham would share the station, but disagreements led to the partnership being abandoned and in 1837 the line was instead extended to Paddington. Opened in 1838, the Great Western's first London terminus was a temporary affair, with four platforms and a wooden train shed.

Brunel was unhappy that the GWR did not have a grand London station, but a lack of finance meant that the company could not build a terminus that matched the rest of the railway for almost sixteen years. The new station completed in 1854 was inspired by Paxton's Crystal Palace and consisted of three wrought iron roof spans. The train shed was designed by Brunel, working with Mathew Digby-Wyatt, who was responsible for much of the decorative work. This stunning design provided enough capacity until 1913, when growing traffic necessitated

PADDINGTON STATION. G.W.R.

The bustling platforms of Brunel's Paddington Station, recorded on an Edwardian postcard. On the right-hand side of the picture, horse-drawn cabs can be seen, awaiting passengers arriving at the terminus. (Author's collection)

the construction of an additional span, in steel rather than wrought iron. While the station was modernised in the 1930s, and updated more recently, it retains many original features. In 1854 the Great Western Royal Hotel was opened in Praed Street, adjoining the terminus; Brunel, busy elsewhere, was not the architect, the younger Hardwick responsible instead for its design.

Waterloo, built in 1848 for the London & South Western Railway, replaced an earlier terminus of 1838 built for the London & Southampton line. The original station was designed by Sir William Tite and had only three platforms; it was extended as traffic grew in 1860, 1878 and 1885. Much of the original station was swept away when a redevelopment took place between 1900 and 1922 – a scheme that included slum clearance and the demolition of a local church. The result was a station said to be the largest and busiest in the United Kingdom. The train shed has a transverse ridge and furrow roof and the station has a grand Edwardian style frontage whose main feature is the Victory Arch – a war memorial to railway staff killed in both world wars. From 1994 to 2007, two platforms became known as 'Waterloo International' and were the London terminus for Channel Tunnel services before St Pancras took over that role.

Kings Cross, opened in 1852, has been described as being one of the most functionally simple stations in the capital. The architect Lewis Cubitt designed the terminal for the Great Northern Railway with assistance from his son Joseph. The frontage consisted of a simple brick screen, pierced by two semi-circular openings, separated by an Italianate styled clock tower. Behind this were two train sheds – one for arrivals and one for departures; the roofs were initially constructed of laminated wood, but these were replaced by wrought iron in 1887. Growing traffic led to Kings Cross being expanded, with two original platforms growing to eight and additional accommodation also being provided for suburban traffic. In later years the front of the station was scarred by an ugly concourse and an entrance to the Underground. In 2012 this was demolished during a £500 million redevelopment of the

The vast bulk of Waterloo Station, viewed from a nearby office block in 2008. The two platforms used for Channel Tunnel services until their move to St Pancras can be seen nearest to the camera. (Hugh Llewellyn)

station that included restoration of the train shed and the construction of a new departures building featuring a stunning roof design by John McAslan.

Victoria was next in date order to be constructed and housed not one but two stations for rival companies – the London, Brighton & South Coast Railway (LBSCR) and the London, Chatham & Dover Railway (LCDR). This led to complicated arrangements and complex architecture; the six-platform Brighton line station opened in 1860 along with an adjacent hotel while the Chatham company completed their terminus next door two years later. In 1898 the LBSCR began rebuilding its facilities to the designs of its engineer Charles Morgan. The frontage was constructed in brick and Portland stone, and the station also had a new entrance in Buckingham Palace Road, used for royal arrivals and departures.

The LCDR was amalgamated with the South Eastern in 1899 and the new company was compelled to invest money at Victoria, which by this time was very run down. The design of the Edwardian frontage was more restrained than that of its neighbour but distinctive enough to distance itself from its rival next door. After grouping, the Southern Railway was finally able to unify the stations, enabling passengers to move freely between the two.

The history of two termini built for the South Eastern Railway are closely linked. Charing Cross and Cannon Street were both opened within two years of each other between 1864 and 1866 and designed by engineer Sir John Hawkshaw; both survive, but a combination of misfortune and redevelopment means that neither retains substantial original features.

The stunning new roof designed by John McAslan, covering the departures concourse at Kings Cross Station, completed in 2012. (Hugh Llewellyn)

The eastern side of Victoria Station pictured in July 1975. A 4-VEP (Class 423) unit waits to depart the terminus. (Hugh Llewellyn)

The frontage of Fenchurch Street Station looks rather scruffy in the view taken in April 1976. The station has been refurbished in more recent years and is now surrounded by high-rise office buildings. (Hugh Llewellyn)

Cannon Street consisted of a 700-foot-long train shed that at the end facing River Thames had two striking stone towers containing water tanks. Betjeman believed their design mirrored that of churches built by Christopher Wren two centuries before; at the city end was an Italianate style hotel designed by E. M. Barry. After being damaged during the Second World War, Hawkshaw's train shed and the hotel were demolished in the early 1960s, leaving the towers standing in splendid isolation. Despite threats of demolition they survive, as does the station, although it now sits beneath a massive office development.

Did you know?

Fenchurch Street Station is probably the least well-known and smallest termini in London. The first station was built for the London & Blackwall Railway and was designed by Sir William Tite; it was rebuilt in 1854 when the L&B joined with the Eastern Counties Railway to become the London, Tilbury & Southend Railway. This new station had a 105-foot vaulted overall roof and two further platforms were added to the two provided originally. The station has always suffered from overcrowding and has been rebuilt a number of times.

Charing Cross also featured a large hotel designed by Barry that opened a year after the station in 1865. The 164-foot-wide train shed dramatically collapsed in December 1905, killing six people; the entire roof was subsequently replaced with a conventional ridge and furrow design that survived until 1990, when an office and shopping complex was built over the platforms.

The arrival of the Midland Railway into London was late and its directors were determined that its new terminus at St Pancras should make a bold statement. William Henry Barlow's 100-foot-high train shed had a cast-iron roof manufactured by the Butterley Iron Company and was notable that it had no internal columns for support. The structure was braced at first floor level by over 2,000 girders resting on a grid of 800 cast-iron columns; the space below served as a warehouse for beer carried by the train from Burton-on-Trent.

The original Hawkshaw-designed train shed at Charing Cross, pictured before 1905, when the roof catastrophically collapsed. Of interest are the ornate gas lamps and the wooden platforms. (STEAM: Museum of the Great Western Railway)

If the train shed was not impressive enough, the Midland employed architect Gilbert Scott to design a hotel fronting Euston Road to eclipse anything yet built by its rivals. Work did not begin on what became known as the Midland Grand Hotel until the station was completed in 1868 and was not finished until 1873. The 500-room hotel was built in the grandest Gothic style and has divided opinion since it first welcomed guests. Described by one historian as 'pompous window-dressing', its clock tower, spires and ostentatious exterior make it one of the most distinctive railway buildings in the world.

By 1972, when Betjeman called it a 'masterpiece', the building was in poor condition, although its Grade 1 listing had removed the threat of demolition. The rebirth of the hotel and the station did not come until 2001, when work began on the redevelopment of St Pancras to enable it to become the terminus for Channel Tunnel services. An additional flat-roofed train shed was constructed for Eurostar trains and passenger facilities for international services were built below the station. Reopened as St Pancras International in 2007, the terminal also handles Midland main line, Thameslink and South Eastern services. The restoration and conversion of Scott's hotel involved conserving and redeveloping the building to house both

The north end of St Pancras Station, photographed before work began on the modernisation of the station as part of its conversion into an international terminal for cross-channel trains. An additional new roof now covers the area shown in the picture. (Paul Childs)

An interior view of the former Midland Grand Hotel at St Pancras taken in 2008, before restoration work began. (Paul Childs)

a new hotel and apartments, and the St Pancras Renaissance London Hotel and an apartment complex were finally completed in 2011.

Later than St Pancras was Liverpool Street; opened in 1875 and designed by Edward Wilson the complex initially included a large 'L'-shaped Gothic building, behind which stood a four-span train shed. In the 1890s it was further extended; with eighteen platforms it was the largest station in the capital, losing this accolade to Victoria in 1908. The station suffered air raid damage in both world wars, but continued to be one of the busiest in the capital. By the 1970s the complex arrangements led British Rail to consider demolishing it as part of a scheme that involved the nearby Broad Street Station. A public enquiry recommended retention of the train shed and in the 1980s a major redevelopment of the station took place, simplifying its layout. Liverpool Street was formally reopened in 1991, and today handles more than 123 million passengers every year.

Did you know?

Broad Street, located close to Liverpool Street, is one of London's lost stations. It was opened in 1865 as the terminus of the North London Railway serving commuter lines in the north and east of the capital. Traffic on the railway was progressively diminished by the growth of bus and underground services, so that even by the 1920s passenger numbers were declining. Damaged by bombing in both World Wars, despite being earmarked for closure by Beeching, trains did not finally stopping running there until 1986.

The exterior of the now-closed Broad Street Station in the late Victorian period. The station also provided the inspiration for the 1984 film and record by Paul McCartney *Give My Regards to Broad Street*. (Author's Collection)

The exterior of London's Marylebone Station seen in March 2008. The fine steel and glass *porte-cochère* provided protection for passengers arriving and departing at the Great Central Railway terminal. (Hugh Llewellyn)

Marylebone was the last London terminus to be completed. Sir Edward Watkin's Great Central Railway made its entrance into the capital in 1899 – a bold scheme to link London and Manchester with a new main line via Nottingham and Sheffield. As the railway arrived late, land was expensive, and as a result Marylebone is more compact, with an elegant red brick and terracotta station building and a cast-iron *porte-cochère*. It was originally to have eight platforms, but lack of funding and traffic led to only four being used. Following the closure of the GCR main line in 1962, the future of the station seemed uncertain; in 1984 BR announced plans to close Marylebone, but these were abandoned in 1986. The fortunes of the station changed however, with the expansion of Chiltern line services to Banbury and Birmingham Snow Hill, and in 2006 two new platforms were added.

4
Metropolitan Glory

The train sheds built in nineteenth-century London were not just confined to the capital. As Britain's railway network expanded, many cities were provided with large stations that reflected not only the importance of the railway companies that built them, but also the status and importance of the places they served.

Many larger city stations were replacements for smaller structures that had been adequate in the pioneering days of railways, but had become too cramped to cope with demand. Nowhere was this better illustrated than at Bristol, where Brunel's original terminus soon proved to be too small despite its magnificent overall roof. In 1841 both the GWR line to London and the separate Bristol & Exeter Railway were opened, but passengers for the latter travelled from a modest wooden station built at right-angles to Brunel's original terminus. The situation was complicated further by the arrival of Midland Railway trains in 1854 and South Wales services some years later.

By 1865 the situation was intolerable and the GWR, Bristol & Exeter and Midland companies joined to build a new station, although it took twelve years to complete the project. The new Temple Meads was built on the site of the old B&E station and designed by Sir Matthew Digby Wyatt, who had assisted Brunel at Paddington. At 125 feet wide, the curved train shed was larger than Paddington, and the Gothic station that housed booking offices for each of the

The joint station at Bristol Temple Meads. The main station building was badly damaged in the Second World War by incendiary bombs, leading to the removal of the tall roof over the clock tower seen in this photograph. (STEAM: Museum of the Great Western Railway)

Art Deco tiling installed when the station was rebuilt in the 1930s has been preserved in the subway at Cardiff Central, and is seen here in January 2015. (Author's Collection)

three companies also featured a large clock tower. Completed in 1878, the station rapidly became congested as traffic developed further, and it was not until the early 1930s that Temple Meads was further remodelled and expanded.

Across the Bristol Channel, Cardiff Central station retains much evidence of its extensive rebuilding in the 1930s. The original station opened in 1850 had been designed by Brunel for the South Wales Railway. The tangled network of railway companies in South Wales meant that the GWR did not have a monopoly over traffic in the Welsh capital and its station was one of two in the centre of the city, along with the Taff Vale Railway's Queen Street terminal. In 1923 the TVR was absorbed by the Great Western along with other Welsh lines, and the GWR station was renamed Cardiff General the following year.

The Great Western did not have the funds to update the station until 1932 when more than £800,000 was provided through government loans. Much of the original station was swept away, and an elegant Art Deco building was constructed housing a booking hall, cloakrooms and luggage facilities. Longer platforms accessed by a new subway were provided and the nearby Riverside Station was also rebuilt to handle suburban traffic from Barry. In 1973 the station was renamed yet again and called Cardiff Central; today the station handles more than 13 million passengers annually and long-term proposals to expand facilities were announced in 2015.

The two largest stations in Birmingham were situated at New Street and Snow Hill and both have had long and chequered histories. New Street, built for the LNWR in 1854, replaced the London & Birmingham terminus at Curzon Street. Although Stephenson designed the station and its layout, the most impressive feature – its overall roof – was the work of William Cowper; the train shed was said to be the largest in the world until the completion of St Pancras.

New Street suffered extensive damage during the Second World War and after 1945 the train shed was removed and temporary awnings were built to protect passengers from the elements. The rest of the station was demolished between 1964 and 1967 when it was completely rebuilt by British Rail. A gloomy new station that was largely underground replaced the airy interior of the original; a concrete deck covered most of the twelve platforms and with the loss of 'air rights' a shopping centre was also built above the station.

Work taking place to rebuild Birmingham New Street Station in the early 1960s. Beyond the two workmen in the foreground there appears much still to do. The rebuilding was not finally completed until March 1967. (Ben Brooksbank/Creative Commons)

New Street's cramped layout and ugly architecture meant that it was disliked by critics and travellers alike. In 2010 work began on a £388 million redevelopment and by 2015 the station was back in business with a new entrance, larger concourse and domed atrium providing more natural light and improved access to platforms.

The Great Western did not gain proper access to Birmingham until 1852 when it opened a station at Snow Hill serving trains from Oxford, Wolverhampton and the Black Country. The first station was a temporary wooden structure that was replaced within twenty years. The new terminal built in 1871 consisted of a single-span iron roof covering two platforms and was described as being a 'dark and dismal place'. With two lines running in and out of Snow Hill, set in a cutting surrounded by busy streets, the task facing GWR engineers in 1910 as they began rebuilding was daunting. The end result was however spectacular. Twice the size of the old station, the new Snow Hill featured two enormous island platforms covered by a ridge and furrow roof. Closed in 1972, it was demolished five years later but a new station was reopened on the site in 1987, although it is now situated under a multi-storey car park.

The station at Newcastle remains one of the finest examples of Victorian railway engineering in Britain. Central Station, designed by local architect John Dobson, featured an iron-arched train shed with curved ribs that would become a pattern for subsequent designs elsewhere. There were three roof spans, each 60 foot wide, supported by cast-iron columns; its size and facilities meant that it was not extended further until 1893 when two further roof spans were added. Plans for a grand station frontage were scaled down when directors decided to move the headquarters of the North Eastern to York, but a grand portico by Prosser completed in 1865 is still an imposing entrance to the station.

Passengers queue to buy tickets at one of the new platform booking offices at Birmingham Snow Hill Station, not long after its completion in 1913. After Paddington, the Great Western Railway's main Birmingham terminal was one of its largest stations. (STEAM: Museum of the Great Western Railway)

The impressive frontage of Newcastle Central Station, pictured in May 2011. The original entrance portico by architect John Dobson was not built as the railway company decided to move their headquarters to York, but the one finally created by Thomas Prosser is nevertheless built on a grand scale. (Railway Heritage Trust/Paul Childs)

York Station.— East Coast Express Leaving.

A Great Northern Railway Ivatt 'Atlantic' class locomotive is about to depart from York Station in this early twentieth-century postcard view. (STEAM: Museum of the Great Western Railway)

Did you know?

The great station at York completed in 1877 replaced an earlier terminus by G.T. Andrews for the York & North Midland Railway built over forty years earlier. Designed by Thomas Prosser and William Peachey, the station has a curved four-span roof reminiscent of Newcastle Central, but its construction is subtler and more sophisticated. As railway historian Gordon Biddle noted, the station frontage is 'very dull', overshadowed by the station hotel next door, and the drama confined to its interior.

Over the Pennines, both the original termini at each end of the Liverpool & Manchester Railway were eventually replaced by grander and more substantial structures. The Crown Street terminus in Liverpool lasted only six years before a new larger wooden station was built at Lime Street. Enlarged by the addition of an overall iron roof covering all three platforms in 1849, by 1867 when the railway had become part of the LNWR a third, even bigger station was built with a large two-span glazed roof. The front of the station was completely dwarfed by the addition in 1871 of the enormous bulk of the North Western Hotel, designed by Alfred Waterhouse, also responsible for the Natural History Museum in London.

Manchester's Liverpool Road Station had closed by 1844, by which time it had begun to handle traffic from the London & Birmingham and Grand Junction railways. A new terminal at Manchester Victoria designed by Stephenson replaced Liverpool Road; in 1909 it was rebuilt and enlarged by the Lancashire & Yorkshire Railway. The Edwardian-style station is

The modern lines of the concourse of Leeds Station can be seen in this 2008 view. Created in 1938 to the design of LMS architect William Hamlyn, the new station incorporated two older terminals – Leeds New and Leeds Wellington. (Hugh Llewellyn)

The impressive 1867 train sheds at Liverpool Lime Street, pictured in 2011. In front of these can be seen the massive bulk of what was known as the North Western Hotel, designed by Alfred Waterhouse and completed in 1871. (Railway Heritage Trust/ Paul Childs)

The new train shed at Manchester Victoria, photographed in April 2016, a year after its completion as part of a £50 million redevelopment of the whole station complex. (Railway Heritage Trust)

An ex-Caledonian Railway '439' class 0-4-4 tank locomotive stands outside the graceful train shed arches of Glasgow St Enoch Station in the years before the closure of this much-loved terminus. (Sid Richards Collections)

one of the best surviving examples of its type; a long four-storey façade retains a canopy that lists the main destinations served by the LYR and inside art nouveau tiling and decoration still survive. Two train sheds sit behind, and at one time Victoria was linked to the now closed LNWR Exchange station next door by a common platform that, at 2,194 feet, was the longest in Britain. A decision to make the station a hub for local and regional services in the North West led to a major £44 million redevelopment of the station between 2013 and 2015.

Did you know?

The main railway terminal for Manchester is now Piccadilly although arguably the most impressive station in the city is no longer used for its original purpose. Central Station was constructed by the Cheshire Lines Committee (a grouping that included the Midland, Great Central and Great Northern railways) and completed in 1880. It had a single-span roof that was slightly smaller than St Pancras, but unlike that terminus it did not have an impressive frontage. The temporary wooden structure survived until the closure of the station in 1969. Manchester Central was largely disused until it was purchased by Greater Manchester Council and converted into an exhibition centre and concert venue. Originally named G-Mex, its railway origins were finally recognised in 2007 when it was renamed Manchester Central.

The exterior of Glasgow Central Station, built by the Caledonian Railway. The entrance is fronted by the imposing hotel, completed in 1883 and extended between 1901 and 1906. (Hugh Llewellyn)

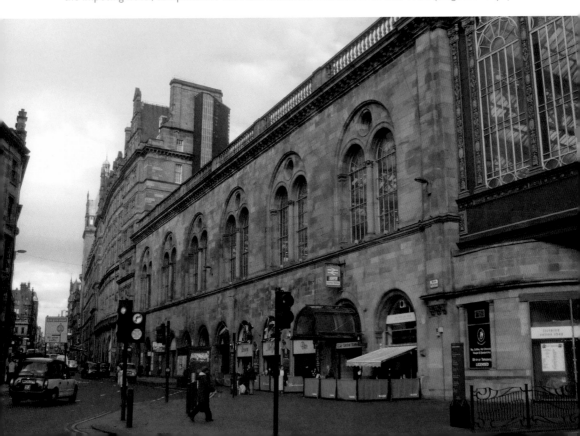

North of the border, redevelopment and rationalisation has seen the demise of some significant major city stations. The loss of St Enoch station in Glasgow was keenly felt; the twelve-platform station had two elegant iron and glass train sheds and, despite handling 250 trains a day, was closed in 1966. Glasgow Central opened in 1879 and greatly extended in the Edwardian period and was the terminus for trains run by the Caledonian Railway. The concourse is spacious and airy, due largely to a large-span steel ridge and furrow roof that removes the needs for supporting columns. The entrance is dominated by a five-storey hotel designed by Sir Robert Anderson in what one writer described as 'French Chateau' style. The smaller of Glasgow's termini is Queen Street, opened in 1842 but rebuilt for the North British Railway in 1877. The single-span train shed designed by engineer James Carswell – the last of its type in Scotland – is impressive and in the style of St Enoch with a glass screen at each end; much altered, the frontage on George Square has now been hidden by new development.

In Edinburgh, the design and architecture of Waverley station are a reflection of its location; situated in the shadow of the castle and between the Old and New towns, when rebuilt by the North British Railway between 1899 and 1902 it was completed with little frontage, attention instead concentrated its interior design. Its nineteen platforms protected by a massive ridge and furrow roof have been described as being like 'a vast array of greenhouses' by railway historian Gordon Biddle.

The entrance to Edinburgh's Waverley station is only just visible on the extreme right of this postcard view. Instead the view is dominated by the vast bulk of the North British Hotel, completed for that company in 1902 to the designs of Hamilton and Beattie. (Author's Collection)

5
Municipal Pride

Between the large and impressive stations in major cities and those on smaller rural and suburban lines were a group of medium-sized stations serving places like county, market or university towns, industrial centres, ports, spas and holiday resorts. Despite the more modest size of many of these stations, there was no lack of variety in terms of architectural design or building material. As was the case in bigger cities, stations could be a manifestation of civic pride and their construction in the heart of a town a focus for urban development. However, this was not always the case, and for railways built later in the nineteenth century, stations might be situated further away from the centre, either because of high land values or outright opposition from civic authorities.

In the case of Huddersfield, its architecture was an affirmation of the importance of the railway and its neoclassical design fitted well into a town square being remodelled at the time of the Huddersfield & Manchester Railway's arrival there in 1847. A local architect J. P. Pritchett was employed and his design, reminiscent of a country house, included a substantial central portico featuring Corinthian columns, behind which a refreshment room was located, linked to smaller flanking porticos housing booking offices. Careful conservation and investment has ensured that Huddersfield's description by many as one the finest regional stations in the country is well deserved.

Another local architect, Thomas Moore, was responsible for the design of Monkwearmouth in Northumberland. The neoclassical central portico is similar to Huddersfield, although smaller and featuring Ionic columns. Completed in 1848, Biddle describes it as a 'noble folly' – its grand design somewhat out of character with the relatively small community it served. Built as a terminus on the banks of the Wear opposite Sunderland, it was originally the nearest station to that town, but with the opening of a railway bridge in 1878 its importance waned.

Few would argue that the neo-classical frontage at Huddersfield is one of the finest railway buildings in Britain. The Grade I listed station was completed in 1850 for the LNWR and LYR. (Railway Heritage Trust/ Paul Childs)

By the time Brunel's Great Western Railway reached Bath in 1840, the city's reputation as a spa had waned somewhat from its Georgian heyday. Nevertheless, the engineer made considerable efforts to ensure his new line blended with the Regency architecture. His station was next to the River Avon on an awkward site with the railway situated on a viaduct. The building and approach were designed to match its location at the end of a street leading from the centre and mullioned windows pierced the main façade constructed in the Jacobean style. Platforms were accessed by stairs and ramps and until 1897 passengers were protected from the elements by a roof built in the same style as Bristol.

The design of Bath's second major railway station, completed in 1870, is arguably of a better quality. Green Park Station, known as Bath Queen Square until 1951, was the terminus of the Midland Railway and also the departure point for trains using the Somerset & Dorset Railway to Bournemouth. The station building is an elegant tribute to the Georgian city with a well-proportioned façade featuring Ionic columns and a simple cast-iron *port-cochère*. Behind, the Midland built a single-span train shed covering two platforms and four tracks. Following closure in 1966, the future of the station seemed uncertain, but in 1982 it was incorporated into a supermarket complex and is now home to shops, restaurants and an events space.

I. K. Brunel's station at Bath. This photograph was taken in 2012, recording the support of the Railway Heritage Trust in funding the refurbishment of the entrance canopy, which was originally added to Brunel's frontage in the late 1870s. (Railway Heritage Trust/Paul Childs)

The elegant station built for the Midland Railway in Bath at Queen Square (later known as Green Park) is fitting of a city full of Georgian grandeur. (Hugh Llewellyn)

Like Bath, Leamington Spa owed much of its prosperity to its growth as a spa resort. The railway arrived in the town in 1852 when the GWR opened its line from Birmingham to Oxford and the new station featured a large wooden roof along with rather plain brick and timber buildings. By the 1930s the station was looking very scruffy and in 1938 the spa town finally got a station befitting its status. A new 'Art Deco' building by P. E. Culverhouse was constructed; steel framed and faced with limestone, it also had stylish walnut-panelled refreshment and waiting rooms on the platforms, restored and updated in recent years.

Did you know?

Great Malvern was well-established as a spa town by the time the Worcester & Hereford Railway arrived in the 1860s. The station, designed by architect E. W. Emslie, was completed in 1862 and while its single-storey Gothic frontage constructed of local stone is impressive, its decorated platform canopies are the jewel in the crown. Each column capital shows a different flower or leaf and is colourfully painted, adding to the charm of the station.

Above: This sketch illustrates the station proposed by the Great Western Railway for Leamington Spa and was reproduced in the company magazine some months before building work began. (Author's Collection)
Right: Beyond the ornate gas lamp in the foreground, the decorated cast-iron station awnings can be seen on the platforms of Great Malvern Station. (Railway Heritage Trust/ Paul Childs)

Like spas and resorts inland, seaside towns and ports grew increasingly important in the nineteenth century and the provision of well-designed facilities for holidaymakers and travellers was important to railway companies. The railway arrived in the fashionable resort of Brighton in 1841 and the station had a grand entrance building designed by David Mocatta. The elegant Italianate brick building was covered in stucco, mimicking the architecture of the seaside town down the hill; it still survives, but is lost behind a cast-iron canopy built in the 1880s and absorbed into a greatly expanded station that includes a fine train shed built in 1883.

Down the coast at Eastbourne, development of the resort took place later than Brighton, and although the railway arrived in 1849, it was almost forty years before it received a station suited to the more respectable visitors that graced it. Situated at a discreet distance from the promenade, the station finally completed in 1886 is a wonderful mix of architectural styles. Blending French Renaissance and Italianate, the terminus is built in yellow brick and its asymmetric design includes a domed roof pavilion on one side, separated by a corner clock tower from the booking hall.

The London & Southampton Railway was the second intercity line to be completed following the London & Birmingham and the port was linked to London as early as May 1840. Sir William Tite, the line's architect, would go on to be one of the most famous and prolific railway designers of his era and was also responsible for stations at Carlisle, Salisbury and Windsor. His station is an exercise in restrained neoclassical design and the three-storey stuccoed building remained as the terminus for passengers travelling on ocean liners calling at the port, while Southampton West (now known as Southampton Central), opened in 1895, handled other traffic for the town. Closed in 1966, the station still survives as a casino.

Tite was also responsible for the design for the terminus at Gosport. The simple train shed was overshadowed by a rather grander Portland stone classical colonnade of fourteen bays linked to an entrance building not unlike that of Southampton. Badly damaged in a

The train sheds at Brighton form the backdrop to a Railway Correspondence & Travel Society rail tour that took place on 13 April 1958. The locomotive is 'King Arthur' class No. 30796 *Sir Dodinas le Savage*. (STEAM: Museum of the Great Western Railway)

Southampton West Station, originally built in 1895 for the LSWR, was completely rebuilt in 1935 by the Southern and renamed Southampton Central. The striking curves of the Art Deco concrete, glass and metal structure were no doubt designed to echo the curves of the liners that called at the South Coast port in those years. (Railway Heritage Trust/Paul Childs)

Sir William Tite's picturesque LSWR station at Windsor. The tower marking the special waiting room reserved for travelling royalty can be seen on the extreme right of this 2009 photograph. (Hugh Llewellyn)

Second World War air raid, Gosport was closed in 1953, and after years of disuse was finally converted into a residential and office complex in 2006. Queen Victoria used Gosport when travelling to her holiday home on the Isle of Wight and she was also provided with a private waiting room at Windsor & Eton Riverside Station, built for the London & South Western Railway in 1849. Like Brunel, Tite could build in a variety of styles and Windsor, in contrast to other neoclassical designs, was a red brick-built terminus in the Tudor style. Careful to create a station that blended in with the surroundings of the town of Windsor and its castle, the main building has an oriel window, arched porch for passengers and a long wall ending with the private waiting room provided for the monarch. It was said that a bell tower on top of the waiting room was used as a vantage point for staff awaiting the approach of royal travellers.

The GWR made much use of red brick in the stations it built in the latter part of the nineteenth and early twentieth century – not just in prominent locations such as Slough or Reading, but also in more utilitarian designs such as the stations built for the new 'cut-off' lines it constructed in the West Country and its new route to Birmingham. The Midland also produced some fine buildings during this period, many using brick and terracotta; over a period of nearly a decade it rebuilt three of its major stations at Leicester, Nottingham and Sheffield in differing styles, all sharing similar types of frontages featuring a large cab area with arcaded walls.

Despite now being overshadowed by rather taller modern offices, the tower completing the façade of Leicester's London Road Station is still a fitting and elegant feature of the 1892 Midland building. (Railway Heritage Trust)

Like Leicester, Nottingham's Midland Station rebuilt in 1904 to the designs of Charles Trubshaw also had a fine clock tower. The tower can be seen through the glass of a cab porte-cochère restored in recent years with support from the Railway Heritage Trust. (Railway Heritage Trust/Paul Childs)

Leicester London Road was reconstructed between 1892 and 1895 to the design of Charles Trubshaw. The station has a long red brick frontage decorated with terracotta, broken by numerous openings for pedestrians and cabs; at one end is a hexagonal clock tower with a 'pepper pot' cupola. Variously described as 'florid' and 'exuberant' by historians, Leicester is full of ornate decoration, whether it is the fourteen urns sitting on top of the frontage parapet, or the art nouveau lettering on the arrivals and departures arches. Nottingham, completed in 1904, was also the work of Trubshaw and was inspired by stations he had seen on a visit to the United States some years earlier. Like Leicester, there is an impressive façade of banded terracotta behind which cab facilities were housed, the ensemble described by Biddle as being 'ostentatious and proudly Edwardian'.

Sheffield's Midland station, also rebuilt in 1904, used stone instead of brick and terracotta for its new frontage. The existing station had become too small to cope with growing traffic and was extended to the west, with the original building remaining as part of the complex on an island platform. Steven Parissien calls the arcade fronting the station 'colossal'; the twelve bays of the screen leading into the building proper provide accommodation for cabs and other vehicles.

Did you know?

'The coming of the railway to Cambridge would be highly displeasing to both God and myself,' noted a Master of Magdalene College before the railway arrived. When it did in 1845, the station designed by Francis Thompson was a fine structure – a fifteen-arch *port-cochère* dominating the approach, the arms of various colleges incorporated into the façade. A long single platform was provided, covered by a colonnaded train shed. This is long gone, but the long platform, capable of holding two trains, survives.

There is a fine array of 1970s taxis evident in this view of the frontage of Cambridge Station. Above the arches can be seen the arms of many of the university town's most distinguished colleges. (Hugh Llewellyn)

Looking more like church or school, the Gothic station at Battle in Sussex is pictured in April 2015. (Railway Heritage Trust/Paul Childs)

In contrast to the standardised schemes adopted by railways for stations in their construction or rebuilding, smaller town stations provide an amazing variety of building styles, materials and layouts. At Battle, on the South Eastern's Hastings line, architect William Tress produced a building worthy of a Gothic novel, featuring an exterior designed to reflect the nearby Battle Abbey and a booking hall more redolent of a Victorian mansion than a station. The Somerset town of Frome was served by the Wilts, Somerset & Weymouth Railway, a company that always struggled for financial stability. The station designed by its engineer Hannaford in 1850 provided a neat and economic solution to the difficulties faced by the company. The overall roof was of a standard design, supported on one side by the station building and on the other by wooden columns.

6
Country and Suburban Stations

Before the Beeching axe cut deep it was estimated that there were more than 5,000 stations in country areas in an assortment of all shapes, sizes and styles; naturally built on a less flamboyant scale than their metropolitan counterparts, they were no less important to the communities they served. The sheer number of rural stations meant that it is harder to find a common design, although many styles such as Gothic, Italianate and Tudor were utilised, albeit on a modest scale. While architects like Brunel and Tite did design smaller country stations, by the latter part of the nineteenth century many were likely to be the products of the civil engineers' department of individual railway companies, and to be of a more standardised design than those produced earlier in the century.

Some broad characteristics can be identified. Initially, at least, stations in rural areas were more likely to be constructed from local building stone, although by the 1890s the relative cheapness of brick, and the ease with which it could be transported by rail, meant that it was used more widely. Not surprisingly, wayside, suburban or branch line stations tended to be built on a domestic scale; in the early days this may well have been because companies wished to reassure the 'timid traveller' by providing them with buildings with familiar shapes, as a contrast to the revolutionary new engines hauling the trains.

Corrour station on the North British Railway's West Highland line to Fort William is a very remote location, ten miles from the nearest road but opened in 1894 to serve the estate of Sir John Stirling-Maxwell over which the railway ran. (Railway Heritage Trust/Paul Childs)

Ridgmont Station, built in 1846 for the London & Birmingham Railway and situated on the line between Bedford and Bletchley, is a good example of the cottage orné style. (Railway Heritage Trust/ Paul Childs)

This view of Horton-in-Ribblesdale illustrates very clearly the standard building style adopted by the Midland Railway for the stations it constructed on the Settle & Carlisle Railway. (Railway Heritage Trust/ Paul Childs)

Charlbury Station in Oxfordshire was built for the Oxford, Worcester & Wolverhampton Railway and completed in 1853. The Grade II listed Brunel building on the up side is seen 164 years later in April 2017. (Author's Collection)

A common pattern was that of the 'cottage' style. The main building usually housed a booking office and waiting facilities, as well as lavatories and parcels office, and the design could be symmetrical or asymmetrical with cross gables linked by an awning or the main roof. Both one- and two-storey buildings could be provided – the latter often providing accommodation for the stationmaster and his family.

While many rural stations had no discernible company 'house style', many railways did build smaller stations to their own pattern, so that there was some continuity along a particular line. On the Settle & Carlisle Railway, completed in 1876, the Midland built a series of standardised single-storey station buildings, mostly consisting of two gabled wings separated by a central section housing passenger facilities. Small, medium and large variants were built, with all but Appleby using local freestone.

The Midland was not alone in working in this way; in the south of England the Italianate style was also adapted for use in rural and suburban locations. William Tress, a pupil of Sir William Tite, designed a number of fine neoclassical stations for the South Eastern including Rye in Sussex, described by Biddle as 'one of the most sophisticated of all small stations'. In contrast, another variation on the theme was cottage orné, a style harking back a century to the picturesque movement that featured half-timbered walls and ornate roof bargeboards. Nowhere is this style better demonstrated than in four stations on the Bedford to Bletchley line, built in 1846, of which Fenny Stratford is probably the finest example. This emulation of the 'picturesque' style was also seen on lines on the Welsh borders, most notably in Shropshire where the Shrewsbury & Chester Railway employed it at locations such as Baschurch, where the station designed by Thomas Penson featured an elaborate turret.

Although Brunel is best known for large stations like Bristol and Paddington, he also produced a series of standard designs for smaller locations. Few of these 'chalet' and 'roadside' stations remain, since many were swept away when lines were widened, and their compact design made them too small for domestic use. Brunel produced a number of variations of both types; built in brick, timber, flint or limestone, the 'chalet' style had a steeper pitch of roof than the 'roadside' design, but both included a characteristic awning to protect passengers from the rain.

Did you know?

Branch lines often featured a variety of station architecture. Most began at larger junction stations whose layouts were often modified as branches were added, as was the case at Kemble on the Swindon–Gloucester line. Wayside stations on branches tended to be small and modestly built, with the terminus being the most important location on the line, often housing not only a goods shed and yard, but often a shed for the branch locomotive.

A large number of country stations were built in the Tudor style; although differing in design across the country, they were often characterised by buildings with tall chimneys and steeply gabled roofs with decorated bargeboards. The small Lincolnshire town of Stamford has two examples of Tudor designs, both reflecting the medieval heritage of their surroundings. Stamford Town, built in 1848 for the Midland, was built to resemble a manor house, complete with bell tower. Still serving trains on the Birmingham to Peterborough line, it is complemented by the now closed Stamford East – a later 1856 station constructed as the terminus of a Great Northern branch line from Essendine.

In the late Victorian and Edwardian period, a number of railways built stations influenced by the new Arts and Crafts Movement. While exponents of that movement like Ruskin and Morris had little time for railways and the world they represented, architects nevertheless produced stations whose designs owed much to earlier vernacular styles and their building materials with hanging clay wall tiles, timber framing and terracotta tiles.

Although timber had been used to construct many early stations, in later years its use as a building material was largely, but not exclusively, confined to places where traffic was lighter or when railway finances were tight. On the London & North Western Railway, standard wooden buildings were introduced that were cheap and quick to build. These modular structures were used all over the system from the 1860s onwards at remote rural locations and larger locations such as Prestatyn on the North Wales coast. The South Eastern & Chatham Railway also made extensive use of timber, building what became known as 'Kentish Clapboard'; the nature of the building material has not surprisingly meant that only a few station buildings of this type still survive.

The Tudor design of Stamford Station in Lincolnshire is clearly shown, despite all the modern signage and less sympathetic modern brick additions that have spoilt the original façade somewhat. (Railway Heritage Trust)

Fairford was the final station on the East Gloucestershire Railway, opened in 1873. It was not originally intended to be the terminus of the line, but lack of finance prevented further expansion. This view taken in GWR days illustrates many features of the country station including small goods shed, signal box and gardens tended by staff. (STEAM: Museum of the Great Western Railway)

The West Highland Railway, opened by the North British Railway in 1894, and its extension to Mallaig, opened seven years later, was one of the last major new routes opened in Britain, and many of its stations – especially those in remote locations – were constructed largely of timber. Designed by J. H. Renton, they were built in what might be called the 'Swiss' style, with brick bases topped by timber buildings hung with wooden shingles. Many also featured a distinctive concave roof design provided to give waiting passengers some protection from the elements. Although some locations had two platforms, in places like Crianlarich and Glenfinnan a more economic island platform arrangement was used.

Did you know?

In rural areas the station was a central part of the community, linking it with the outside world and enabling agricultural produce to be sent to markets in cities. In some cases, stations were located not in the centre of a village, but some miles away; this might have been due to opposition from local landowners when railways were planned, or parsimonious railway engineers wishing to avoid expensive earthworks in areas where the terrain was unfriendly. Invariably, such stations often had the name 'Road' added to the destination – a tell-tale sign that passengers might have a long walk to their destination when stepping off the train!

The Swiss chalet influence can be clearly seen in this modern view of Rannoch Station on the West Highland Railway. (Railway Heritage Trust/Paul Childs)

In the early part of the twentieth century railways, in an effort to generate income and compete with bus and tram services in rural and suburban areas, introduced the new concept of 'Halts'. These stations were the smallest to be built on the network, and were usually built cheaply; most consisted of one or two short platforms constructed of timber and usually provided with a simple hut to offer protection for waiting passengers. The Great Western were pioneers in the field, and by 1914 had more than 160 in rural, suburban and main line locations.

The grime, congestion, and poor quality of housing in urban areas led to the development of new housing on the outskirts of many large towns and cities, and the growth of railway services to cope with the increasing numbers of people wishing to live there. While railways did not directly create new suburbs, they nevertheless supported their growth; as well as providing more trains, they also built new stations and improved existing ones to cope with additional traffic. As early as the 1860s railways in London had been building additional smaller but impressive stations on commuter routes such as Denmark Hill, built for the LBSCR in 1866. Its Italianate booking hall was badly damaged by fire in 1980 but is has been rebuilt and restored in recent years.

In the years between the two world wars further development of suburban stations was undertaken largely by the Southern Railway and London Underground. There is not space here to chronicle all the work done by the London Passenger Transport Board in this period but the influence of General Manager Frank Pick and architect Charles Holden led to the introduction of a standard building style. Before 1925, engineers had designed stations rather than architects but the commissioning of Holden led to the development of a corporate style that included architecture, lettering and advertising. New Art Deco-style stations were created on the Central, District and Piccadilly lines and existing ones updated elsewhere; the effect was completed by attention being paid to features such as lighting, benches and ticket machines so that the overall effect was modern and stylish.

The halt built by the GWR to serve the golf course at Denham had corrugated iron 'Pagoda' sheds not only on the platform, but also utilised to act as a small ticket office. (Railway Heritage Trust)

Above: Commuter grandeur. Originally built by the London, Brighton & South Coast Railway as York Road in May 1867, Battersea Park finally acquired that name in 1885 and was designed by architect Charles Driver. The rather theatrical interior features some fine cast iron columns. (Railway Heritage Trust/Paul Childs)
Below: Despite looking a little neglected, the Art Deco lines of Holden's Chiswick Park Underground station still look modern, even on a dull day in April 2017. (Author's Collection)

The new terminus at Portishead in Somerset completed in 1954 by British Railways replacing an earlier station dating from 1867. The Beeching Axe meant that it lasted only ten years and was subsequently used as a garage. (STEAM: Museum of the Great Western Railway)

On the Southern, the programme of electrification on its suburban network led to the construction of what it called 'ultra-modern' stations and the upgrading of existing facilities. As well as rebuilding larger urban terminals at places like Ramsgate and Hastings, the company also built modern stations that must have seemed alien to the commuters using them. Chessington North, completed in 1938, featured a stark brick station building with a tower. The platforms were accessed by stairs and covered by ribbed concrete shelters that were a world away from the traditional steel and glass structures usually provided for passengers. Surbiton was completely rebuilt in 1937, and while its Art Deco styling make it look more like a cinema than a station, its modernist design still looks current today.

7
Station Life

By the 1930s, each of the 'Big Four' railways were responsible for a large number of stations that varied from the largest and most imposing metropolitan termini to the smallest wayside station and halt, and much in between. The largest station on the GWR was Paddington, which employed almost 1,400 staff and earned the company more than £2 million annually; Oxford, one of its middle-sized stations, had a staff of 189 and an annual income of £150,000, while the nearby Culham station with 10 staff only earned £1,839.

Away from city terminals, stations elsewhere shared many common facilities and buildings that were familiar to the travelling public until the Beeching cuts and modernisation of British Railways. In contrast to today, when travel tickets can be bought online or from machines at stations, for more than a century passengers purchased their tickets from a booking office. At small wayside stations this could be just a small pigeonhole, behind which a porter or booking clerk sold tickets, or a purpose-built booking hall at larger locations.

Awaiting the arrival of their train, if they did not wish to sit on a draughty platform, the passenger would have had the choice of waiting rooms of varying quality, usually dependent on the class of ticket purchased. Railway catering has always been a subject of some contention among the travelling public, and it is no exaggeration to say that standards of fare have varied widely across the network from the earliest days of railways to the present. As early as the 1840s complaints were being made about the quality of catering at Swindon and Wolverton and in

Culham, a good example of a surviving 'Chalet'-style Brunel station building. Situated on the Didcot–Oxford line, the station is still in use, although the building is not used to sell tickets. (Author's Collection)

At many larger stations, a bookstall was provided for passengers. The first example of a bookstall was opened by William Henry Smith at Euston in 1848. By the time this image of Paddington was taken, early in the twentieth century, the company had moved into the high street, prompted by rent increases from railways like the GWR and LNWR. (Author's Collection)

1866 Charles Dickens' short story 'Mugby Junction' chronicled his travails at a refreshment room where soup and tea were virtually indistinguishable. By the end of the nineteenth century standards had improved, and many larger stations in particular had grand and spacious dining rooms that served food of the highest quality. Betjeman described the Windsor Bar at Waterloo as 'Edwardian deluxe style at its most refined'; by the 1930s more modern Art Deco-style snack bar dining was available, providing food for those with more modest budgets.

Did you know?

Railways had helped establish a uniform time for the country soon after their widespread introduction in the 1840s and the importance of timekeeping was reflected in the number of clocks that would have been seen by railway passengers. As well as familiar English drop dial clocks that might have been visible in the booking office, many stations also featured much larger public clocks inside and outside the main building. In a time when not all people owned their own clocks and watches, these timepieces were an important part of the lives of local people and travellers alike.

Right: The grand surroundings of the Centurion Bar at Newcastle Station which was originally the first class refreshment rooms. Although the rooms were built when the station originally opened in 1850, they were improved in 1893 by the North Eastern Railway when the walls, arches and columns were covered in Burmantoft tiles. (Railway Heritage Trust/ Paul Childs)

Below: Station clocks like this one, situated at Paddock Wood in Kent, were a common feature of stations in the nineteenth and early twentieth centuries. (Railway Heritage Trust)

For many travellers, the railway hotel would have been a familiar sight, particularly before the end of the steam era. The first railway company to introduce its own dedicated hotel was the London & Birmingham, who provided accommodation at Euston and Curzon Street, Birmingham, in the late 1830s. The completion of Hardwick's Great Western Royal Hotel at Paddington and the Great Northern Hotel at Kings Cross in 1854 was followed by a period of sustained building in both the capital and further afield. Ultimately, only Blackfriars, Fenchurch Street and Waterloo did not have their own hotels, but in many major cities where several railways competed for traffic, they often built large hotels close to their stations.

Nowhere was this more apparent than in Birmingham where both the Great Western and LNWR provided accommodation at Snow Hill and New Street respectively; in Liverpool, the massive hotel provided by the LNWR at Lime Street in 1871 was eventually matched by the Midland's Adelphi, bought by the company in 1892 and rebuilt between 1911 and 1914. Whereas the North Western Hotel was originally decorated in the French Renaissance style, its Midland counterpart owed much to the influence of the Ritz.

Another common feature of a station, whether large or small, was the signal box. These familiar structures began appearing on railways in the 1860s, although before that signalmen and other staff had operated signals and points from lineside huts or platforms in the open. The development of both the electric telegraph and signal and point interlocking greatly improved the safe working of trains, especially on the busiest lines, and signal boxes were a by-product of these improvements, providing accommodation for both signal staff and the increasingly sophisticated equipment used. The most common design for boxes was two-storey, with signalmen housed at first floor level, giving them an excellent view of the running lines and station. Accessed by a flight of stairs, inside the cabin was the signal lever frame, block instruments and other staff facilities such as a toilet, while below was a room containing the interlocking mechanism and other safety equipment. The design of boxes and

A postcard view of the station hotel at Birmingham. This grand structure stood close to the city's New Street terminal, which can be seen to the right of the hotel. (Author's Collection)

Snow Hill Station, Birmingham

Birmingham Snow Hill (GWR) - 9

The grand entrance to Birmingham's other city terminal at Snow Hill. The overall roof of the station stretches down Livery Street on the left of this postcard view. (Author's Collection)

their building materials varied enormously from company to company and place to place; brick, masonry and wood were all used in combination.

The traditional design continued to be built, even in the 1930s, although by that time railways were beginning to introduce newer designs often utilising more modern materials such as brick and concrete. The Southern Railway in particular built stylish new brick boxes nicknamed 'Queen Mary' or 'Odeon' by staff that featured a large base that also provided accommodation for track staff, with a top section complete with curved windows giving a good view of the railway. During the Second World War, boxes were built to government standards that made them more resistant to damage during air raids with reinforced roofs. With the introduction of colour light signalling, the design of boxes changed further; the rise of power signal boxes and regional centres controlling long stretches of railway has meant that the days of the old signal box are numbered. Plans announced by Network Rail in 2011 noted that with the concentration of all signalling in fourteen centres, all remaining mechanical boxes would be closed – the majority within fifteen years.

While passenger traffic remained – the more glamorous side of the business for railway companies – it was goods traffic that in most cases provided the bulk of their income. With the exception of the largest metropolitan stations that had little in the way of goods provision, most stations had a goods yard with sidings and a goods shed or warehouse. The sheer variety of items moved meant that staff could handle many and varied goods; as a 'common carrier', unlike road hauliers, railways could not refuse to carry a load when offered.

Above: The signal box at Helsby Junction, which is situated on the Chester to Warrington Line. The box is a standard LNWR design and was built in 1900 to replace another elsewhere at the station; it has now been listed Grade II by English Heritage. (Railway Heritage Trust/Paul Childs)

Below: The GWR goods yard at Hullavington. A loaded wagon of hay stands on the weighbridge, while a horse box waits in the bay siding in the foreground. In the distance, milk churns stand close to the cattle pens. (STEAM: Museum of the Great Western Railway)

Did you know?

Until the coming of road and rail tankers, milk traffic was still a large and important part of railway business. In the 1930s railways worked with larger dairy companies to build milk depots in large cities to service the ever-growing demand for milk. Until this time, large urban stations had handled thousands of milk churns each day – full churns being loaded at country stations and brought to cities by rail, with empties returned later in the day.

Most goods sheds were of a utilitarian design, containing a platform and crane for unloading loads from wagons as well as a dock where horse-drawn and motor vehicles could be loaded. In larger town and city locations, railways built larger depots, often with additional floors above the transhipment space that allowed goods to be stored before being moved elsewhere. Outside in the goods yard there was normally provision for the unloading of cattle and other livestock; until the 1930s, much of the shunting in yards was still done by horse, and so stabling facilities were also usually a feature in both large and small stations.

Many railway stations feature war memorials dedicated to the large numbers of staff killed in the two World Wars. This example at Manchester Victoria sits beneath an enormous tiled map of the Lancashire & Yorkshire Railway system. (Railway Heritage Trust/ Paul Childs)

8
What Now?

Despite some important losses, a significant legacy of station buildings still survives, both in railway operation and in new uses. As well as being able to visit these locations, there is a wealth of other information for those wanting to find out more.

Further Reading

Biddle, Gordon and Nock, O. S.: *The Railway Heritage of Britain* (London: Michael Joseph, 1983) The first definitive guide to Britain's stations and other railway heritage.

Biddle, Gordon: *Britain's Historic Railway Buildings: A Gazetteer of Structures and Sites* (London: Ian Allan, 2011) A comprehensive survey of over 2,300 of Britain's historic railway structures.

Betjeman, John: *London's Historic Railway Stations* (London: John Murray, 1972) Written at a time when heritage was still undervalued and under threat from railway management, with evocative photographs by John Gay, it is still a classic.

Cromford Station was built for the Manchester, Buxton, Matlock & Midland Railway and completed in 1849. The ornate buildings are thought to have been designed by G. H. Stokes, son-in-law of Joseph Paxton of Crystal Palace fame. (Railway Heritage Trust)

Binney, Marcus & Pearce, David: *Railway Architecture* (London: Bloomsbury Press, 1979)
A series of essays on railway stations and railway heritage written by architects and
conservationists.

Fawcett, Bill: *Railway Architecture* (London: Shire Books, 2015) An excellent, concise
introduction to the subject.

Hendry, Robert: *British Railway Station Architecture in Colour* (Hersham: Ian Allan, 2007)
Packed with colour images, this book chronicles the development of stations from the
earliest days.

Meeks, Carroll: *The Railroad Station* (New York: Yale University Press, 1956) Although
published more than fifty years ago, Meeks' book was the first serious book about railway
architecture and remains a classic.

Parissien, Steven: *The English Railway Station* (Swindon: English Heritage, 2016) An
accessible and well-illustrated survey of the architecture and social history of railway
stations in England.

York, Trevor: *Victorian Railway Stations* (Newbury: Countryside Press, 2015) Well illustrated
with both photographs and the authors own detailed drawings, the book tells the story of
stations in the nineteenth century.

A First Great Western 'Adelante' stands at Platform 1 of Brunel's Paddington station on 3 April 2006.
(Author's collection)

Web Resources

There are literally hundreds of websites on railway topics, and while there are few specifically dedicated to railway stations, many have information about them. Many sites for individual heritage railways include historic material as well as current information about services.

The Railway Heritage Trust was established in 1985. Funded by Network Rail and Highways England (Historical Railway Estate), its objectives are to assist in the conservation and upkeep of their listed buildings and structures on the national railways, and to assist in the transfer of non-operational building and structures from the national railways to outside bodies willing to undertake their preservation. With a budget of £2.2 million it provides grants to enable national railway buildings and other structures to be conserved, and also provides specialist advice to planning authorities, architects and others to help conserve, and find new uses for Britain's railway heritage. Copies of the Trust's informative annual reports can be downloaded from its website. www.railwayheritagetrust.co.uk

Historic England is the public body that looks after England's historic environment including its railway architecture. Its website contains information and research about listed stations and access to its archive of historic images and archive material. www.historicengland.org.uk

An invaluable online database of railway stations that have closed in the UK can be found at: www.disused-stations.org.uk; each entry has historical data and images, maps and pictures showing what remains.

The website of the National Railway Museum at York is not only packed with information about the 1 million objects the museum has in its collection, but also contains useful links and blogs. www.nrm.org.uk/

Chester was a joint station built in 1848 for the Chester & Holyhead and Shrewsbury & Chester railways. The architect Francis Thompson provided a grand Italianate frontage that has been well restored in recent years. (Railway Heritage Trust)

Museums

There are a number of museums whose collections include the story of railway stations. Please check opening times before visiting!

London Transport Museum, Wellington Street, London, WC2E 7BB
Tel: 0207 379 6344
www.ltmuseum.co.uk

National Railway Museum, Leeman Road, York, YO24 4XJ
Tel: 08448 153139
www.nrm.org.uk

STEAM: Museum of the Great Western Railway, Firefly Avenue, Swindon, SN2 2EY
Tel: 01793 466646
www.steam-museum.org.uk

Stations to Visit

A large number of stations mentioned in this book are still operational and it is possible to visit many of them. There is not space to individually list stations here but both Gordon

Hertford East, a terminus of a branch line on the old GER main line to Cambridge, was rebuilt in 1888. The fine brick building features no less than two *port-cochère* structures. (Railway Heritage Trust./Paul Childs)

Biddle's *Gazetteer* and Trevor York's *Victorian Stations* are good sources of information. Please note that some operational stations may only be accessible with a valid ticket for travel; some may also have restrictions on photography. Other stations may have new uses as business premises or private homes, so please take care when visiting.

Heritage Railways

Listed below are just some of the British heritage railways that retain interesting original railway stations as part of their operation. A full list of railways can be found on the website of the Heritage Railways Association. www.heritagerailways.com/ or the heritage railway guide at heritage-railways.com

The Bluebell Railway, Sheffield Park Station, East Sussex, TN22 3QL
Tel: 01825 720800
www.bluebell-railway.com

Gloucester & Warwickshire Railway, The Station, Toddington, Gloucestershire, GL54 5DT
Tel: 01242 621405
www.gwsr.com

Great Central Railway, Loughborough Station, Leicestershire, LE11 1RW
Tel: 01509 632323
wwwgcrailway.co.uk

Keighley and Worth Valley Railway, The Railway Station, Haworth, West Yorkshire, BD22 8NJ.
Tel: 01535 645214
www.kwvr.co.uk

The Mid-Hants Railway, The Railway Station, Alresford, Hampshire, SO24 9JG
Tel: 01962 733810
www.watercressline.co.uk

North Yorkshire Moors Railway, Pickering Station, North Yorkshire, YO18 7AJ
www.nymr.co.uk

Severn Valley Railway, Kidderminster Station, Worcestershire, DY10 1QR
Tel: 01562 757900
www.svr.co.uk

West Somerset Railway, The Railway Station, Minehead, Somerset, TA24 5BG
Tel: 01643 704996
www.westsomersetrailway.vticket.co.uk

Station architecture often features standard equipment common to most locations. Some oddities were provided by architects; this incredibly ornate drinking fountain can be found at Pitlochry Station in Scotland. (Railway Heritage Trust/Paul Childs)

This station clock at London Kings Cross was originally located on a footbridge at the terminus. The recent redevelopment of the station saw the replacement of the bridge and its relocation to the Mid Hants Railway. The clock has however been relocated on the west wall of platform 8 at Kings Cross. (Railway Heritage Trust/Paul Childs)